Shores of Freedom

Contents

Features

Every year, families in the United States and Canada celebrate Thanksgiving. Read how this celebration started on page 9.

Would you have enjoyed living in colonial times? Learn about a busy colonial day in **From Dawn to Dusk** on page 14.

Who became famous because of a poem about his horse ride through the night? Find out on page 25.

Discover a changing world in **The World in the Late 1700s** on page 28.

Who was Pocahontas?

Visit www.rigbyinfoquest.com
for more about EARLY COLONIES.

New Horizons

In the 1600s, life was very difficult. Cities were dirty and overcrowded, farming methods were poor, and fatal diseases were common. Starvation and **plague** were a constant threat. The 1600s were also a time of rapid change in Europe. Scientists were beginning to discover how the world worked and how the lives of ordinary people could be improved.

PROFILE

Isaac Newton (1642-1727)

The 1600s were a time of important discoveries and new ideas. One great scientist of the time, Isaac Newton, explained the idea of gravity. One day, he saw an apple fall from a tree. This gave him the idea that the gravity that brought the apple to the ground might also be what keeps the moon orbiting Earth.

Some people began to question their leaders and what they were being told. As people got a taste of freedom and choice, they began to hope that their families might have a better future. People in Europe started to think of traveling to new lands in search of freedom and adventure.

When Ferdinand Magellan's crew sailed around the world in 1522, it proved that Earth was indeed round. This was important. It meant that ships could sail in one direction and still get home. Until this time, many people had believed Earth was flat.

The 1492 voyage of Christopher Columbus to the Americas, or the New World as it was then called, was followed by others seeking to discover and claim new lands.

Puritans and Pilgrims

Early in the 1600s, the king of England forced everyone to worship in the same way. This angered a number of religious groups. Some of these people wanted life to be more simple or pure. They became known as the **Puritans**. Some Puritans decided to stay in England and try to bring about changes.

What Do You Think?

Each Pilgrim family on the *Mayflower* was allowed to take one chest with everything a family would need to survive in a new land. They could also take a Bible box containing the family Bible.

What do you think a family would have had in their chest? What would you have taken?

Puritan

Others, such as the **Pilgrims**, looked to the New World for religious freedom. In 1620, one of the Pilgrim ships, the *Mayflower,* set sail for America. It had 102 passengers and took 66 days to reach the New World. The journey was long and difficult, but it set the scene for the creation of a new nation.

Pilgrims say goodbye before boarding the *Mayflower.*

Early Days

The Pilgrims set up a colony called Plymouth in what is now Massachusetts. They built simple houses from timber with roofs of grasses. A fireplace in one wall was used for cooking, heat, and light. The only things people had were the things they brought with them in their chest or what they were able to make.

Today, people can visit **replica** colonial villages, such as this one of Plymouth, and see actors performing typical colonial activities.

About three months after the Pilgrims arrived, they were visited by local Native Americans who showed them where to fish and hunt and how to plant an unfamiliar crop called corn. This helped the new colony to be successful.

In 1621, Governor William Bradford, of Plymouth, invited Native American neighbors to join with the Pilgrims to celebrate and share some of the successful harvest. This was the first Thanksgiving feast in the colonies.

Thanksgiving Day is now celebrated in the United States on the fourth Thursday of November. In Canada, Thanksgiving is celebrated on the second Monday of October.

9

The Thirteen Colonies

Between 1607, when the first successful colony was set up in Virginia, and 1733, thirteen colonies were established in the New World by England and its later union as Britain.

The colonies were set up by different groups with different leaders. Many colonists came because they wanted freedom to worship as they chose. Some came because they wanted to trade and set up new businesses. Some wanted to explore and obtain new land and riches.

The first English settlement in North America was at Jamestown, Virginia. It was named after King James I of England. This photo shows a replica of the seventeenth century village.

SITESEEING · **PAST & FUTURE**

Who was Pocahontas?
Visit **www.rigbyinfoquest.com** for more about **EARLY COLONIES**.

A flag called the Continental Colors was America's first national flag. It combined the British flag and thirteen stripes, one for each colony.

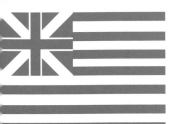

New Hampshire

Massachusetts

New York

Rhode Island

Pennsylvania

Connecticut

Maryland

New Jersey

Delaware

Virginia

North Carolina

South Carolina

Georgia

The Original Thirteen Colonies

Life in a Colony

Life in the first American colonies was very different from life today. The men worked long hours in the fields, clearing, planting, and harvesting. Women worked hard preparing meals and looking after the children. Men and women needed to be skilled in various crafts such as basket making, candle making, and thatching.

The homes were small and dark inside and the kitchen was the main room. There was little furniture in the colonial home. If there was a chair, it was for the man of the house.

PROFILE

William Penn (1644–1718)

William Penn founded the colony of Pennsylvania for a peace-loving group called Quakers. This group had been badly treated in England.

Penn insisted that anyone living in his colony had the right to worship as they chose, and that everyone was treated equally. He made a **treaty** with the local Native Americans that was never broken. The colony of Pennsylvania was the most democratic of all the colonies and one of the most successful.

There were no supermarkets in colonial times. The colonists grew their own fruit, vegetables, and herbs, and they cooked over wood fires. Their homes were built using local materials.

From Dawn to Dusk

Today, we take our lifestyle for granted. Flick a switch and the lights come on, turn the faucet and hot water rushes out, press a few buttons and the microwave heats food. Life was very different for the colonists.

When the sun came up, the family first had a breakfast of corn mush, meat, and cheese. Then they attended to their daily chores, which often filled the whole day. Here are some activities during a normal colonial day.

All building was done by hand, and people often had to help each other. The main building material was wood, which was plentiful in the surrounding forests. Here, two men are sawing planks of wood to build a house.

Feeling hungry? How about having a biscuit? First the flour must be ground from wheat, rye, and oats grown in the fields. The dough is then baked in an outdoor oven or in an iron container over the fire. Children were often given the task of chopping wood to keep the fires going.

Most households owned a few goats, cattle, hogs, and chickens. The animals were used for food, clothing, and labor. Cheese and butter were made from goats' milk.

15

Colonial Children

Children were highly regarded in colonial times. Their labor was important to the well-being of the family. Most colonial families were large, and many had six or more children. Unfortunately, large families were necessary because many children died then from measles and other diseases for which we now have cures.

Boys wore dresses until they were about six. Then they were old enough to help in the fields and dressed just like their fathers. Girls dressed like their mothers. From the time they were quite small, they learned to sew and to help with chores in the house.

Colonial children had to work hard. How many different chores can you find and name in this illustration?

School Days

The colonies set up schools where children could learn to read and write when they were not needed at home. There were not many books, and most learning was done by memorizing the lessons.

This building in St. Augustine, Florida, is the oldest wooden schoolhouse in the United States.

French and British Battles

Even before the British began settling the East Coast of America, the French were settling the northern and southern shores of the Saint Lawrence River. Early in the 1600s, fur traders set up trading posts. Farmers came with their families to start new lives in the colony of New France. By 1750, the French were competing with the British in many parts of the world.

Samuel de Champlain (1567–1635)

Born in France, Samuel de Champlain explored many parts of the North American coast, the St. Lawrence River, and the Great Lakes region.

In 1608, Champlain founded Quebec, along the St. Lawrence River, as a fur-trading post. This was the first permanent settlement of New France and was to become the center of French power in the colonies. Champlain's maps, drawings, and books are a valuable record of the early days of New France.

France and Britain both wanted control of the fur trade in North America. In 1759, the British army won a battle against the French army at Quebec. In 1763 with the Treaty of Paris, almost all of New France became part of British North America.

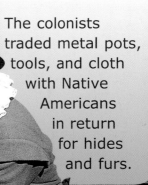

The colonists traded metal pots, tools, and cloth with Native Americans in return for hides and furs.

Displaced People

Many early French settlers moved to Acadia (now the Atlantic provinces of Canada). They fished, farmed, and traded with the local Native Americans. The British and French armies were often fighting in the area, and the lives of the Acadians were seldom peaceful! In the 1750s, the British took over Acadia. The British didn't trust the Acadians and wanted them to leave. The British burned their farms and broke up their families.

Acadia

Gulf of St. Lawrence

Quebec

New France

Thirteen colonies

Let the Good Times Roll

Cajun music and food is enjoyed by many people today. The popular fiddle and accordian music is lively. The food is rich, spicy, and delicious. Even the names of the food— jambalaya, etoufee, and crayfish pie—can be exciting.

Many Acadians fled and built new communities around the edges of the Gulf of St. Lawrence. Over the years, many made their way south to Louisiana, in the Mississippi Valley region, where their **descendants** live today. These people are called Cajuns, which is a another form of the word *Acadia*. Many Cajuns speak French, just like people living in the Canadian province of Quebec.

New Orleans, Louisiana

From Colony to Nation

Throughout the 1700s, the settlers in the thirteen colonies became more and more frustrated with British rule. Many colonists did not agree with some laws made by the British government. The colonists were forced to pay taxes to pay for Britain's wars with France. More and more British soldiers arrived to enforce the tax laws.

The Boston Tea Party
December 16, 1773

The British East India Company had much more tea than they could sell in Britain. They decided to sell it cheaply to the colonists. This meant the colonial merchants could no longer make a profit.

Some colonies prevented the tea from arriving in their ports. However, three ships did reach Boston. Samuel Adams and over one hundred other colonists dressed up as Mohawk Indians. They boarded the ships and dumped the tea into the harbor.

As a protest, the colonists refused to buy any goods imported from Britain. All thirteen colonies were united in their wish to keep their new-found freedoms. Finally, tension between the soldiers and the colonists resulted in the Boston Massacre on May 5, 1770, in which five colonists were killed. Mistrust and opposition to British rule continued to grow.

The Power of Words

Newspaper articles and circulars helped fuel growing unrest. Phillis Wheatley wrote **patriotic** poems that were widely read. Wheatley was kidnapped as a child in Africa and taken to the colonies on a slave ship. She was a servant to a Boston tailor.

Revolution Brewing

Until 1770, the fight between the colonists and the British was mostly a war of words. That changed with the Boston Massacre and the Tea Party. Anger against the British grew. In the countryside surrounding Boston, groups of armed colonists prepared to fight for **independence**.

On the night of April 18, 1775, British soldiers quietly marched out of Boston. Colonial leaders guessed that the British soldiers were planning to seize the colonists' gunpowder and other **military** supplies. That night, two patriot riders named Paul Revere and William Dawes were sent on different routes to warn colonists throughout the countryside. When the British arrived in Lexington the next day, armed colonists were waiting for them. The American Revolution had begun.

Revere engraved a number of political cartoons, including this famous though incorrect poster of the Boston Massacre.

PROFILE

Paul Revere
(1734-1818)

Paul Revere was a silversmith who worked in his family business in Boston. He became famous for his patriotic activities. Revere took part in the Boston Tea Party and was often a special messenger for the Boston patriots.
He became a hero for his most famous ride on April 18, 1775, as remembered in Longfellow's popular poem.

. . . So through the night
  rode Paul Revere;
And so through the night
  went his cry of alarm
To every Middlesex village and farm,
A cry of defiance, and not of fear,
A voice in the darkness, a knock
  at the door,
And a word that shall echo for
  evermore!

From "Paul Revere's Ride" by Henry Wadsworth Longfellow

A Changing World

While Britain was fighting to hold onto its colonies in America, the kings and queens of other European nations watched closely. The rulers of Spain and Portugal had American colonies, too. They hoped that their colonists would not fight for independence. France hoped its old enemy Britain would be defeated, and it sided with the thirteen colonies.

In 1788, a British **penal colony** was set up in the newly-claimed colony of Australia.

Meanwhile, explorers continued to visit countries never before seen by people in Britain. The British explorer Captain James Cook explored the Pacific. He mapped the east coast of Australia and the islands of Tahiti and New Zealand. Australia and New Zealand both soon became colonies of Britain.

Convicts were sent to jails in Sydney and Tasmania, Australia, because prisons in Britain were overcrowded. Many of the convicts had been sent for crimes as small as stealing a loaf of bread. In Australia, they were given hard labor constructing roads and many buildings.

The World in the Late 1700s

Canada

Britain wins Canada from France in 1763.

France

The French Revolution takes place in 1792, and King Louis XVI is beheaded.

Western America

Spain rules much of the land west of the Mississippi River.

American Colonies

The American colonies win independence from Britain (1775–1783).

Central and South America

Charles III of Spain rules all these lands except Brazil.

Brazil

The Portuguese have a rich colony in Brazil.

West Africa

Millions of Africans are taken as slaves for Europeans in North and South America.

Prussia

King Frederick the Great rules Prussia (now Germany), which is one of Europe's great powers.

Russia

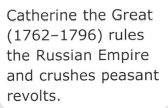

Catherine the Great (1762–1796) rules the Russian Empire and crushes peasant revolts.

China

China's tea trade with Europe grows.

Turkey

Turkey is part of the Ottoman Empire that covers parts of Europe and the Middle East.

Japan

Japan refuses to trade with Europeans and is cut off from the changing world.

India

Britain does not rule India but influences its politics and economy through its trade with India.

Australia

British explorer James Cook explores the Pacific (1768–1779) and becomes the first European to see a kangaroo.

Glossary

convict – a person who is in prison because he or she has committed a crime

descendant – a person who has a certain ancestor. Your descendants will be your children, their children, and so on into the future.

independence – freedom from being controlled by other people or governments

military – having to do with soldiers, armed forces, or war

patriotic – to show great love and loyalty for one's country. A patriot is a person who is patriotic.

penal colony – a settlement outside a country where the country sends some of its prisoners

Pilgrim – one of the English settlers who left England seeking religious freedom. The Pilgrims started a colony in Plymouth, Massachusetts, in 1620.

plague – a disease that spreads quickly from person to person and often causes death

Puritan – one of a religious group in England in the 1500s and 1600s. The Puritans wanted simple church services and a strict way of life. Many moved to America in the 1600s.

replica – an exact copy of something

treaty – a formal agreement between two or more countries that has to do with cooperation or trade

Index

Research Starters

1 Imagine you are a colonial child. Have a close look at the illustration on pages 16–17 and write a journal entry of a typical day. Starting with when you wake up, describe the food you eat and your chores throughout the day until bedtime.

2 Find out what food was prepared for the first Thanksgiving meal. Who did the Pilgrims invite, and why? Do you think Thanksgiving in 1621 would have been more enjoyable than the Thanksgiving we celebrate today? Why or why not?

3 The 1600s were a time of new ideas and important discoveries. Galileo Galilei, William Harvey, and Isaac Newton made important findings. Research and discuss why their discoveries were important.

4 Who are your ancestors? What do you know about your great-grandparents and great-great-grandparents? Draw your family tree and include where each person was born. Try to get more information from your family, books, or the Internet.